8/16

M000289925

$\mathcal{P}$ARTS OF THE MASS

Catherine Imbriglio

PARTS OF THE MASS

Burning Deck/Anyart, Providence, RI

Grateful acknowledgement to the editors of the following publications where versions of these poems first appeared:
American Letters & Commentary ("Communion" [under the title "Exegesis"]); *Brown Literary Review* ("Agnus Dei," "Christe"); *Conjunctions* ("Psalm," "Recitative" ["A photograph"]); *Denver Quarterly* ("In Nomine"); *Epoch* ("Sanctus," "Vere Dignum Et Justum Est"); *Pleiades* ("Epistle 1-4").
Grateful acknowledgement also to Reginald Shepherd for publishing "In Nomine," "Psalm," "Gospel According to the Middle," "Gospel According to One Who Always Needs an Audience," and "Gospel According to How We Throw Stones," in his *Iowa Anthology of New American Poetries.*

The author wishes to thank the Rhode Island State Council on the Arts for a merit award in poetry.

Special thanks to Nancy Donegan, Michael Harper, Mei-mei Berssenbrugge, Lee Teverow, Marjorie Milligan, Mary Gavin, Rebecca Kanost, Sandra Moran, Keith and Rosmarie Waldrop, Gale Nelson, and most especially, for all his inspiration, encouragement and unwavering support, Reginald Shepherd.

This book was made possible by a generous gift in memory of Toni Warren.

Burning Deck Press is the Literature Program of ANYART: CONTEMPORARY ARTS CENTER, a tax-exempt (501c3), non-profit organization.

The cover uses a detail of aquatint #2 from "7 Black Poems" by Irene A. Lawrence.

© 2007 by Catherine Imbriglio
ISBN 978-1-886224-81-0 original paperback
ISBN 978-1-886224-82-7 original paperback, signed edition

for Genevieve and Adam Imbriglio

TABLE OF CONTENTS

PARTS OF THE MASS

Say for me.

Say forth, say forthwith, in the name of colors, of real colors, in the name of real colors named, in the initial real color named, say Brunelleschi, say curvature, say Sir Francis Crick. For what we are about to receive, not only show all fragile passengers, red in the initial appearance of a material surface, say this is the place, this is the effort on our part, this is where we'd say, "This is." To expend our dream hoard that the years ago came from the ancient monotreme lane, enter "the lovely ropemaker," 1520 - 1566. In memory processing, in egg laying, in "let them alone so they'll come home," from to look at, add species hours, add breath toll, add an REM script. To the inquiring name, recognizing it needed room, it needed feet, for some-what as though, it, you, drew, birdscatterer, through the engine of, the stem of, from up to your body breakable, i.e., "if all the trees were one tree." It drew through its tongue, its backwater, its layer upon layer, its layer upon layer beneath the larger layer, for when in your shock upon shock, in the name you were named: be monkfish, be milkwort, be mate.

I will go.

I will go then.

Once consolidated are said. Once safely departed are said. During once which I would never roll my eyes. She was 15 at the time. She was 15 at a garden party. And refused an introduction, and refused the closest the mind comes to, as introduction. As long as we do, we do. The figures how do you do indomitably passed. Other stubbornly irreducible Mabels and of in at 15, their higher mentals functioning. On the ventricle side, holes she said are said, the ventricles in fact, in fact at the rest stop we indomitably. Are one up on the so where and how not welcome at the center of which she thought ventricles without actually detecting anybody. Who are at least one up on who he she thought centered in the cerebrospinal, fine. Restored to a proper body, when in the midbrain geese have long lives. Ventricles are which in fact said. At proof in the invisible accompaniment, once in safely departed, fine. Thought first of objects could have been traced on a windowpane even in. Not to mention a frank possible connection to Descartes' cell. It seems to me, but also the. To be freed of the. To speak of so long and sincere in its willful in its like-minded point of kind. No longer the sweet and beautiful thing it once was. She meant to say, but. Separated from its more thick its more coagulated find.

Lesser dodder = clover dodder
Lesser broomrape = clover broomrape
Lesser celandine = pilewort
Lesser bramble = the dewberry

Lesser hours = little hours
Lesser hemlock = fool's parsley
Lesser spike rush = needle spike rush
Lesser curlew = the whimbrel

Lesser omentum see omentum
Lesser bulb fly see bulb fly
Lesser emerald bird of paradise see bird of paradise
Lesser butcher bird see butcher bird 3: sometimes the reedling

Lesser sciatic foramen see sciatic foramen
Lesser yellowlegs see smaller yellowlegs
Lesser calamint see field balm
Lesser sigmoid notch: look: where the whimbrel

for Reginald Shepherd

I

Each now dropped

Lay your hands upon me, you in the black bent grass, the body in motion that stays in motion, so too in your drifting to or from me, in the pictures of the body that provoke the body, *judica me*, you in the blackpoll warbler, *judica me*, you in the black-tailed godwit. It wasn't on purpose was it, in the way you get it down or keep it down, my texture to your texture, in the body as motion that stays as motion, *judica me*, which one of us, like spit. One of us should try breathing in the mirror, each mirror holding yet another mirror, it *was* something like communication wasn't it, how many persons to a copper or silver goblet, how many persons from holding out their bowls. So too you in this drifting to or from me, in the pictures of the body that provoke the body, let me not from the circulation of impediments, let me not from accommodation to the pose.

II

No internally fixed order of stages stop. Under incremental light conditions stop. I look out and see under the lilacs stop. From wood-bine to woodbine stop. Day unto day one tree frog two duckboards three goat moths stop. Made you look made you look made you look you stop. Were word of godetia real word stop. If without if without finding stop. What impudicity what who me stop. There is stop no speech no language where the voice from the wilderness stop. When it comes a'courtin' and we all go stop. Yours to then yours to wend watch stop. Day unto day while we take its sweet time stop all rise.

III

Spiny wings that, suppose that

Break their teeth with your lips, break the teeth of the dumb flowers,
open wide the calyx, for when you do what you do, I who you your
honor, broke out in teeth, the alleged teeth, for at just that time, admit,
for open wide, admit, were you or were you not, *selah,* down beside me
among the cow wheats, the bull thistles. Go for the throat. Now we see
it, now we, in sun mouth, in ripened seed head, casual, seriatim, party of
the first part wreak party of the second. Rattle the big pharmaceuticals.
Reign in with limit list. Rattle for rattle, rattle *of* rattle, constrained by,
gag ordered, most wanted, grift. So moved. Hoop ash, basket ash, a set
of promises, a mimicry. And then, an if then, a nothing to me. I lost my
place. Partings of the first part beneath a parting of the second. So
moved. Ballast love, when a rain coursing through me. Here. Hearsay.
In here you'd say.

Into the right eye, into the Mare Imbrium,

a fall from symmetry.

On hold, in the hold, what if the mare's nest

what if the open sea

Easters were full course dinners in two rooms. She hated
wearing dresses because all her cousins were boys.
Ripples in the space-time fabric move off in all directions
which would be an equivalent for the laughter emitted
from the rooms. She saved her relatives formally
as if they were jewelry boxes she'd never use.
She wanted them to "do it." The moon somehow got tipped
as if someone believed the best noisemakers were guns.
I can't keep up the kind of waiting necessary between episodes,
even though a bullet shot into the air returns to earth
at nearly the same velocity as when it was fired.
That makes her think the country is numb.

She doesn't know about the velocity of the drops which fell
from the celery her grandmother dipped in water.
Her grandmother said it was "holy water." To celebrate
the season now, she gets some French table wine. The cashier
keeps calling her "young lady." She doesn't correct him because
she is studying the chemistry of the brain. By the fireplace
are chestnuts whose shells have been picked clean.
The remnants look like owls' faces. When I am facing you,
I am wondering about the terminology for the model's eyes.
On the ground, the owls have empty eyes. She bends over them,
but she doesn't say "who" out of politeness, since the chance
of a model working successfully might be even, like at least
one doubling of deathdays if there are 22 people in the room.

She made a great effort to memorize the facade of the building. There were some asters left over and everyone trying to get in to see you. When Nelson saw that other guy's shirt was open he began repeating radio call numbers. It was a kind of hard part, like going into a mirror for a distance of fifteen miles. He told her, You can't give sympathy to anyone expecting a perfect exchange.

Afterwards Andrew said, What do you call a bull who sleeps? She thought it easier to talk about the population of certain grasses which rise and fall rather than the visual machinery which picks out vital signs. She was imagining a requiem. Its Kyrie would be unprotected from radiations by the yellow lenses of the eyes.

The need to tell you, the need to tell anyone,
displaced, handling displacement,
the meal served, the highest point of splendor served,
the snowdrop flowers as is, as it is, like servants,
like low lit lamps bending over February,
over this side of February, over any side, through a failure of contingency
not over until it's over, until it's once and for all
over, like second nature taken in, February,
overcast, overcome, overlord.

———

By this time, having annoyed everybody by not entering the heraldic
functions at the start, the head-first posture altered like the sewn
eyelids of a young hawk, the lazy eye growing on one side of the face
all along, by this time the melisma going off, a hammer at that pitch; it
was striking by means of the half note, the half moon, the half life, the
halter, the second period of mourning, the clothes wearing thin, so that
by this time (see also sediment, sedilia), a river was in her mouth. They
said, Your breath smells of it.

So that she was thinking of the word alignment, more or less graspable,
using objects. Or, spare the water, spare the land. Lastly, of a strong
willed cloth: whom have I forgotten now (see also) the form of a prayer
to fold you.

———

Has it on. Has it on us.
Has it on. Has it on us.
Has. Half. Has.
Has it. Has it any.
Any heart. Any sister.
Any woolens. Any wool.

I

So that each step was to someone like you, as someone selling his soul was to his place in line. So that you could have stayed longer, how sweet, in the suite, the retinue blowing hot and cold, trained, with some measure or reference point so nice you'd come home to, banded, banned, played out, like yellowed ivory, soul distributed, soul magnified. Because of the plane, curled up, fetally, fatally, don't be so stiff, afraid of what they've sucked inside. Truncated, below the belt, actually, agrimony, same as, a mass of distinct things, too crowded to be satisfied, are you satisfied, are you satisfied, the wail-house growing dimmer, the carvings extending them into domesticity not at all, not at all satisfied, but forced, with the transition, to cooperate, to conduct electricity like moisture under the bark where it used to hide.

II

You won't be said, will you, to end it, to figure that it's going against you, to transfer your motive to my motive and mine to yours; meanwhile, along with everything else, the sold soul is leaking apostrophes right through your side. O Danny Boy, from end to end, the spiral in the temple, going down, purified. On my knees, brought to one's knees, targeted, derivative, Miriam, Marietta, Molly, Marilyn, Marion, Maureen, overhead the gulls keep tightening their circle, wanting something from the dead one circled inside.

I knew you back then. Magnificat, the sold soul is kept alive.

III

Consequently, they went their separate ways, burned their candles at both ends, did their own thing, etc., espousing an amorality of means, the momentary aesthetic the sum and substance of value. If you aren't smiling, why not, if actions speak louder than, why do they, if some of the energy expended is absorbed elsewhere, why are you. In much the same way, details in this picture seem to be themselves, candidly. The swallows for each Capistrano, they came back, her virginity for each new john, it came back, the whole body came back like a garden growing; how does it, I said. She was aestheticizing each self contrarily, like a disembodied voice, like an inefficient voice, like history; on those occasions she said, he's history, but he came back, hierarchically he came back, hierarchically he came back licking his fingers clean.

We lean to listen.
We listen to one side.
Any et, et, et, is.
Et in terra.
Et in terror pocks.
Et in terror pocks, ho, "meanie," buss,
bone, eh?, vole, lune, tart, ah!, tis.
Any neck ligament.
Any "to collect the remaining grass."
Any ridged shadow from that glass
as elastic as beau, nay, bonae voluntatis.

Et in era, era, parks.
Et in era, era, parks.
Et in error, error
pax home, mean, he, bus,
bow neigh, veau, loon, tar, art, is.

Of good will. Of their selective good will. Of any
single or doubly long sighs. Of what in common is.
"For every one of them without exception flows
from the state of their possessor's body at the time."

Loud, ah, uh, ah, uh, arm, moose, day, "A."
Loud, ah, uh, ah, uh, I'm, mousse, te, eh?
For every single one of them without exception,
glow, reef, fee, car, muss, te.

———

Glorificamus
the light paths the wind leg marks on the water which are now, suddenly,
before. Glorificamus the light paths which are now suddenly bowlegged or wishboned.
Glorificamus the white light, now separated or dispersed. Glorificamus the wind
spreading the legs of the light paths, like bowlegs or wishbones. Glorificamus
now material hesitation which burns, like the wind spreading
the legs of the light paths, before.

———

With which we, the tongue of a vertebrate or any tongue, "when so many others whom he knew or knew of," by which we, by which we could, birds sidling along a telephone wire displacing each of their neighbors like beads. Thanks to you, clouds form an uneven frieze on the diagonal. Swallow, swallow, o swallow anyone whole. With so many others whom he knew or knew of, before the eagle became the eagle, I thought the machinery behind Mendeleev's table a second order statement, under the birdwoman's whose missing mouth carried one seed.

Hands down, heads down, come down, they all fall, precocial birds, composite birds, in intimate space, they roll the eider down. Rubs down, rubbed them down, in classical space they manage not to collide. Dominoes, dolma, wrecks chair, lest cyst. The moon is upside down. Dressed down, loaded down, thrown up by the wind near the side. Any more I can not wish you, an ancient down, coiled at the base of the spine.

She hands the eider down.

Rest   jay   lest   sis

––––––

Speak low, the sum of square waves or sawtooth waves expressing a
    sine wave.
Speak low, you who insist, finger to finger, the two extremes of its arc.
Speak low, for the eye to tether the moondog, the paraselene.
Speak low, of the window where people were throwing down all sizes
    of paper stars.
Speak low, qui tollis peccata mundi.
Speak low, the necessary but insufficient condition, you who would stray
    from its arc.

To:
From:
Dear:

Pass on, fair god, pass on, for within what is called erosion of material,
pass on, for and if, in the middle of normal or abnormal circumstances,
were you out in public, pretty pretty public, pretty pretty public in.
How beach boy, how oscilloscope, how Audrey Meadows' elbow, I
want you to know brothers and sisters, in the proportional representation
of credent variables, like water under the bridge brothers and sisters,
like New England dog whelk brothers and sisters, if for no other reason
but that he can brothers and sisters, how sea urchin, how beaded
miter, how bottle-head. Verily the glory of the immortal hand, to be
surrounded by, with some sea turtles pressured more than other sea
turtles, for no other reason but that he, how mimmation, how flatboat,
how humble, humble, humble, in.

Do not mix old with new batteries. Do not mix alkaline, standard or
rechargeable batteries. An organism's inherent set of values, do not
mix. Can't reach your sandbar, quote, it was background emotion,
quote, who did you think you were talking to, who did you think
would stumble in. See, see, the goodly cedars. Give me a C. C. Give me
an E. E. Shot full of. I want you to know, brothers and sisters. Who are
themselves varying in their (check one): homeostasis. ten-in-one
rations. mind over matter. bliss.

Yours:
Truly:
Postscript:

Pull pressure. Push pressure. Up pressure. Down.
More bow. Less bow.
Not all one silence.
Not all one sound.

Friday June 8 2001
Brethren:
On behalf of:

The light. The temperature of the light.

The temperature of the light as it rushes in to touch her, touch him.

The spill-over of the bodies taken up where the light begins
to deplete in its fine-grained motion, the invitation to the thing, the once
    more
once over, in the issue of the light that issues in.

As one by one, the beach apples happen.
One by one his lips, her eyes, his skin.
One by one, the waves, the measure of the waves, "so that we may be
    mutually
encouraged by," in the sum of their devotion, the need to pick one, pick this.

Imagine the heat, what he thinks about the heat.
Imagine if you could change things. To be worthy in that veneration,
of the-too-much to take in.

And later that day, a running to the fence, this far away.
Sharp words or no words, why should I tell *you*,
of the millions of things it has to tell, reserved for whom?

For your convenience, in taking out the myth?
The coming together right now?
You can think these things (do something, do whatever he tells you),
    until the thing
that has already happened, postponed in the gift of your abstraction, is
    once again

is once again in the pick one, pick this.

As if in talking to her younger self, the next older self, the one after that,
the next and the next, to the one just seconds past and then
to the coming attraction.

Who she was in that chapel, outside that chapel. As if the question was put
to generate something in her mind just now
about then. The refugees (this man living in this camp for more than twenty
    years, this girl for that camera, for the flooded path, raising up her hem)

the *now* of them

one by one, crowded out in the selective tragedy, one by one crowded out
    in the selective plane.

And you up there, the one with the camera — he she it —
picking at them, the one-by-one's

inside of that story (if you won't do it, who will), on behalf of, brethren,
until once again, brethren, until what then or who — person-to-person,
    brethren —
what then or who are we to say was gained?

As someone speaking to you in hurried terms:

Greetings:

In fixed beginnings, as in chess:

I would have come. I had long intended to come. Past fact, past contrary to fact, past epistemic modality, my tongue, my tongue, what has it done, what has it done to you, each step in time, manhandle, woman-handle, past sea thong, sea whistle, past go-along, fish. Move to the other side. That sign might be shown to be sign, show: I can break down that flight in twenty steps. *I* can break it in two steps. Break it. Break down that flight. Then when we meet. Put. Under "water": Phoebe. A vanishing. Good mood. Good job. Good bait and switch.

I wish I'd said
I could have said
I should or shouldn't have said

You   For

It   To

When three is the point it is called knobbed brain coral.
When four is the point it is called sea whip.
When five is the point it is called stickleback.
When seven is the point it is called red beard sponge.

When eight is the point it is called king's surrender.
When ten is the point it is called deontic.
When eleven is the point it is called you that.
When twelve is the point it is called may or must go.

October 7, 2001
12:35 p.m. EST

Beloved:

Used chiefly, used attributively:

Do this in:

I

Not many days before it, we saw bluefish jumping after some bait fish; wherever there were bait fish we saw turbulence from below and above — below from the blue fish arcing out of the water, above from the terns diving down in; for them, I mean for the blues and terns after the bait fish, for the fishermen after the blues, and for us, in the act of observing, for all of us (except for the bait fish) it was such an easy taking; whenever we saw the bluefish the river looked as if it were boiling; where the water boiled I saw the parts given to the bait fish — silver minnows driven up to the surface and finally to the rocks where we were standing, flat silver slivers driven to the rocks and then onto the rocks, as they tried to escape the frenzy in water and air; several times on different segments of the river we watched this, the birds and the blues and the fishermen after the bait fish, at each segment a replay of that first commotion, all the parts and the performers of the parts moving closer and closer, until the fish and birds (but not the fisher-men) moved into the inlet and we onto the rocks at the water's edge; how terrible it was, that beauty we (he and I) were after, how terrible the noise from all that flapping, the splashing that sounded close to loud applauding, how terrible an entertainment all that death and death's commotion, right in front of us in the inlet between the bridge and the island with the teahouse where in the summers we had seen so many wedding parties (their brides and grooms just across from the bridge and the rocks where we were standing), how terrible in that cause that effect that collateral damaging, so that, from that, how many ways are there to say this, once again we (he and I) could see parts do not have individual properties separate from the main.

Further still, behind us, two white herons — quiet — sat stiffly in the trees.

II

Seven eleven you came for it. Seven eleven, in drizzle light, the intimate remains.

III

IV

A full moon: We are now over

Shall the country: flown against the country: be the country

As it was the: as it ever was the: first the cold snap the cold chisel the cold warrior the cold wave

In the *and* the, in the ever *and* the: I heard now: asymmetrical: in the asymmetrical: in the twenty-six days

World without the: world without the: shall the country flown against the country: I heard now: twice the cold snap the cold chisel: cold warrior: cold wave

With the end the, with it ever end the: shall the country be the country not the country: I heard now: a full moon: in the affliction of the body: time is running out: time is running out: time is

In the beginning: country: in the beginning: country: as it ever was, shall the: as it ever was, shall the: for to whom, in it: country: for to whom, in it: country: as it ever was, shall the: as it ever was, shall the: for to whom, as it: beginning: for to whom, as it: beginning: as it ever was, shall the: as it ever was, shall the: for to whom, whom it country: for to whom, whom it country: in it ever was, shall the: in it ever was, shall the: whom the beginning whom it made

I

A photograph is an index that fractures your mobility.

Odd her oddness, like zero as a place marker, a unit of measure in the
     photograph that's set to anchor in a system of counting.

It says it happened.

It collapses from an interior.

Look at the moments when you say you watch carefully.

Weighing bottle. Salt mouth bottle.

This is the part where evil is subsumed by religiosity. .

It is not a question of whether to pin the towers down or be evocative,
     your mobility consumed by their immobility, you trying to stop you
     from not having to address what's passed.

To describe the excavation, take a photograph and put circles around its
     archaeology.

The numbers in the circles represent a faux interiority, steel, flesh, ash, air.

When you turn the vessel turns.

The flattened picture of the street fills to her reactive body.

At the same time, cordially, you could say, we have a photographic bypass.

It is all in the timing. She assumes the uncaptioned photograph is a retro-
     gressive case shot for military fire.

It is not combinatory, as with a formula, but a depth perception, even
     though "the concept of image-as-opinion is difficult for most people
     to grasp."

In this manner looking is both assault and being assaulted.

We see through that which sees through that.

Some of which I may be imagining.

Its supplies.

Its demands.

II

In her right eye, the degree of visual definition measured along the vertical
    and horizontal axes is unsatisfactory, because a spiked cataract is growing.
The film of the developing cataract distorts her image transfer, as in a
    glut of information, what things her brain selects, sausage, ricotta,
    for a hasty meal preparation.
In the immunity of a photograph, think: you can go now, you can go back in.
Her right eye is her default eye, i.e., her dominant eye, to whose imagery
    the brain submits, so you won't see the stunned woman stunned totally.
Light teases out a latent action in the lens, hope in proximity, what you
    now do or then did.
She anoints herself with such narratives.
Sunspots in her mind's eye correspond to the mating parts of the external
    to the internal thread, as from a table of oils, pressed radially.
She experiences an indwelling, terms she wants to break into, deep fascia,
    deep femoral artery, deep epigastric artery, for a moment of second
    sight that is once again temporary.
That could be me, breaking the window, the third one from the left.
I begin dinner by pouring olive oil into a pan.
I select fish, bread, greens, carrots, candles, wine.
Outside he may be planting.
The light on the cherry trees elaborates the fallen petals of the cherry trees.
As with a waterway, she takes a sounding.
At the extreme point, the incline of a roof, one half pitch, one whole pitch,
    the ratio of the height to the span, like arms around a stranger.
You can pave a street with the rubble, as with a series of undressed stones.
She plays a tape she keeps of beloved voices, here and not here, as if
    sound were a mending instrument.
The voices rise as from a carpet, ash to petal, in degree, number, rate,
    proportion, kind, the force of a transparency.
The voices rise, as from a carpet, blown.
They relay a periphrastic present, a strain on the values of her photo-
    elasticity.

First fog
First fire

First apple
First liar

First lady
First lead

First hardwood
First dead

for Gale Nelson

I

In the beginning was the who, and the world was with who, and the world was who. The beginning was both before and after the who, and because of the beginning, the world could light-hearken, light-hearken to all that it was, to all that could be made. I am not the who but the one who comes across the who. I am the one who separates the singer from these strains. Between us was the string and the lute was with string and the lute was string. And all things come from strings, begotten not made. They were in the middle, not made. Her eccentricity was, on the other hand, made. I have seen it missing, the lute, the middle of the lute, who from the beginning was the one from whom all things were made. From the beginning, the lute was also an if, the one who was with the if, and the one who was if, begotten not made. If the water could be clear, it could be green and scummy, if the water was clear or green and scummy, it was not the lute, it was not the middle of the lute, because in the beginning the lute was an if, and from the beginning, water, yea the water, it could be made.

I say unto you lute, I say unto you light-hearken, I say unto you whom I do not say. She was with me and she was me. It is no longer the beginning. It is the middle and the middle is cruel. I say unto you, through you and in you and with you, you who join with me separately or come together maybe towards dusk, or maybe much earlier, light-heartened, before we go swimming. It is always useful to go back and say you are merely towards dusk, or would have come much earlier, since even before you are after, and before-after is the middle, is the middle where you may be saying, who was that if so light-hardened in its distributions to the brain.

II

"Whereas, once upon a time, I walked along the white cliffs, for miles and miles, getting white chalk on my shoes. When a man hailed me from the brush about 20 yards above, I realized how stupid I was for walking alone. Sometimes I think that in a concurrent life he must have done me in, because even now when I think of it, my feet sweat so as to eventually ruin my shoes."

reception reception money loaves fishes owl rockband children's stories
    reception reception
reception reception money loaves fishes owl rockband children's stories
    reception reception

claim claim reception reception money loaves fishes owl rockband children's
    stories claim claim reception reception
claim claim reception reception money loaves fishes owl rockband children's
    stories claim claim reception reception

reception reception claim claim reception reception claim claim reception
    reception claim claim reception reception

III

Topographical shapes

Irregular masses of gray matter

It is the spirit that gives life, the flesh is useless. This is called begging the blessing. This is called who is kissing who knew. At the asses' bridge (pons asinorum), some basic tests for the inexperienced mathematician. The soft mute, the middle mute, where reason is transacted. Let all numbers be in the set voice, the intermediate voice, between the active and the passive. Let who is kissing who knew. For heightened a little, the lights are combative. You, sit with your pants down until I tell you you can move. The anchorman, citing military wisdom, warns against fighting the "last war," i.e., the previous war, not the one that will end with the earth's extinction. Please stand. Please be seated. Soon I will no longer be speaking to you in figures. The soft mute, the middle mute, where reason is transactive. Let if the spirit give life, the flesh be useless. Let if one brood nest and one brood nest then two. This is called begging the blessing. This is called who is kissing who knew. In a little while and then in a little while. Money loaves fishes reception reception. Money loaves fishes reception who.

She gives it to herself

He gives it to himself

Supposing him at first to be the gardener, half of his plants on one side, half on the other, he taught me how to measure rows with right measure, that the garden was always a garden, meaning, a gamble, back-strength and arm-strength on one side, the elements and wildlife on the other; he used to plow in the mornings, take produce to his wife and all the neighbors in the late afternoons-early evenings; like his brothers and sisters, he was what we used to call bull-headed, not as with his music moderato, as if from dusk to dusk he could win the fields, win at the law of averages; for years, hoe in hand, he managed the weed crawlers and the stink grass, but even so, supposing him at first to be the gardener, I was wrong: when he got old the garden was no longer a garden, meaning, a gesture; so as, I say to you, dusk to dusk, nothing is as it was when he first appeared.

Please stand. Please be seated.

Gospel according to what rises to our consciousness.
Gospel according to temper temper temper tune.
Gospel according to some man's stolen wallet.
Gospel according to how he cleared the room.
Gospel according to false cohosh=the blue cohosh, of Algonquian origin.
Gospel according to how we stand our moods.
Gospel according to y while x is happening.
Gospel according to the sun according to the moon.

Q. *Can one recognize a dream as comic? I mean from inside the dream interpret an image and laugh? Aunt and uncle trying to keep you from leaving by shouting "poison sumac, poison sumac in your path"?*

A. Those who are well have no need of a physician. Through leaching, mother and daughter elements can be swept away. They read the text and predict it will happen. Fifteen young women die in a fire because they aren't properly veiled. Start talking. Don't pass it over. Grapestone, backstone, goatstone, hairstone, milkstone, bird stone, stone root, stone clover. The fault lies not with our scars but with our narratives. Let us play. Let us play out. Pins and needles. A patch of new cloth on an old cloth. Surgery will be done as an outpatient procedure. You sew and sew. Dehiscence. Septicidal. Do you hear me. Do you hear me now.

Q. *So if it's only your dream followed by my dream, of separate cities, separate reconciliations, do you know (and if you do, how do you) are we actually harnessing the stone's throw?*

A. My great uncle sold crushed stone to the city of Fall River which used it to build roads. Whereas "myth does not provide a blueprint for pragmatic political action" (Armstrong). Monsters will be monsters, see me boiling each liquid by dropping in hot stones. Granite for granite, sledge hammered, split (saxifrage grows in stony places): what you know and do not know (the world as weighted weight) is smashable (use grievance grown from grief, as from a foundation of crushed stones). But what if in dreams we're held responsible, hold out your hand, it's nearly night now — for you, here's honey yellow, also known as honey middle stone.

Feeling in some way what these people knew all along, so named in French after the debasement of the French coin, she thought, catkins before the leaves caterwaul, she thought, paper makers of the insect world, not a mean sting, but a nervous sting, with a wasp habit of a fan folding its wings; all day long her intimacy was in French, the abdomen usually marked by crosswise bands or rings, by catkins where you can't see the water any more; all day she thought, you have the wrong Rachel without end, but gladly their nests are made of real paper, of cells they lost: sworn by my daughter's eyes, it was an intimacy which filled the pores, or, if the woman were dead you would love her more; all day she thought, the second stomach of a ruminant, she thought, goose summer with an allusion to a warm period in the fall.

The local garages so multiplied the choice between them,
gaunt, stripped, "given to be seen," the elder Frank
a remarkable little landscape, very pleased
with the prearranged witnesses in the living room.
The maintenance of the canal moving effortlessly
from medium to medium: the leather buckets, the fire dog,
with three to six men at the rest stop all telephoning.
By definition the least complimentary term,
the monstrous ear turning yellow prematurely,
but "not something to take into the theater with you,"
the burnt out landscape, the three years to make a firehorse
unafraid of smoke or the noise.

how energy may not

how an animal with a behavior that changes may not

Meet Mussolini, his hands credibly soft: nothing should impress you,
nothing should adsorb

The quick brown fox jumped over the low wooden fence: a frame or
railing on a ship's table kept the dishes from sliding off

A new and improved means of memory consolidation: there's more,
wait there's more

The ratio of body mass to brain mass: holobenthic, as long as she
doesn't wet the floor

A tight shirt on a sweaty farmhand: he had flashbacks and feared the
consequences of helping the law

Coming soon, August 6 : property of goosegrass, etiquette of grown

I feel better that you feel better: basal ganglia and the cerebellum are
critical for the acquisition of skills

This time when the fruit loops fall the path is visible: dwarf blue, points
to a globe

A fact we all agreed not to acknowledge: a billion Gainsboroughs into
the space of this o

I never should have called him: a figure or design carved beneath the
surface of a stone

This scent a chemical recognition signal: made against water, air

The technical philosophical term is "qualia": who had a short history of taking off her clothes

Insults to the lain upon: for the purpose of removing human will

Tight shut and sweetly flow: in lithographic limestone, feathers as well as bones

Circumference continuous with your ciliary body: how far would you go

Why wait for the cold pill to start working: whey worm, whey matter, whey blooded, whey dawn

Too large to squash into our skulls: in expansion and contraction, there's heat involved

Your ear — is it singing: still thinks of me as a little girl

Perspective cannot see itself: a world not spoken as the world hurries on

Ride a cock horse: random, by virtue of ignorance of a contributing cause

Trained persons open the young oysters: a tobacco pipe usually has two parts

Like swans biting themselves: the concept "equally likely" difficult to grasp

Do I hear one dollar, do I hear five: will not resemble the larger structure they are trying to hide

Falling from the waist, three inverted darts: for Leonardo, the problem of the unrepresentable in both science and art

Now listen, sister: when sheaves formed like this: part of the given by which you give

I

The sought after, the always three degrees away from bloom.

The mean position of the body in proportion to that alignment, that scene.

The world, as it follows them along, following simply, following some do-as-you're-told.

Their attachment, the manner of their attachment, the means.

Meanwhile, the milkweed pods, with their faces pushed in.

Meanwhile, the milkweed pods like dry grey birds which sow each seed with their feathers spread.

Dividing the weight of each body by its acceleration.

In which case the body of the lord.

II

Their attachment to the world is odd, the devices they throw at the world, odd, the voices thrown, the astragali thrown, the o come all ye metacarpus and menhaden, thrown, then when it came to them, the white heron whose neck fit a question or a hook, then when her neck on his shoulder so that it built, according to mass by a percentage in ionic form, in the beginning was spirit gum, in the beginning then was he the most exposed.

III

I.e., this is my body, this is my body, this is yours,

IV

Pressed in the hairs they lost,

V

As in, instrument or means used.

VI

Now something in the world dividing on or off.

Now something in the world on or off then dividing him.

Now something in the world in him then dividing then dividing in.

Now something in the world the most exposed in on or off the divided him.

Now something in the world if then the weight of each window now accelerating.

Now something in the world him weight the window now divided now divided now divided in.

I

Sound waves, in the absence of organs to perceive them, have no sound.

Hearing is her ability to convert and interpret sound waves.

Air on either side of her eardrum must be at equal pressures for her drum to vibrate freely.

In her middle ear, vibrations are amplified by a chain of ossicles.

The last of her ossicles is called the stapes.

The footplate of the stapes, in contact with the oval window of the cochlea, transmits vibrations to fluid in her labyrinth.

Hair cells in the lining of her cochlea vibrating to the different frequencies stimulate her nerve lines.

In the tiny area of the cochlea, she makes thousands of exquisite discriminations.

Vibrations can reach her acoustic nerves through the bony structures in her head, as well as through her ears.

Fluid in the three semicircular canals gives her information about the positions of her body.

Bone conduction is especially related to the way she stands herself speaking.

What she hears begins as "shook-up" air.

A teasing pattern of interlocking elements hears "when the bough breaks" as the balance in the middle term of a syllogism.

Her whole body is shaking.

II

Most of the text of the mass is called ordinary.

Under ordinary conditions, the mass of a body is constant.

The inertial mass of a body is a measure of the body's resistance to acceleration by some external force.

All evidence seems to indicate that the gravitational and inertial masses of a body are equal.

Music as a mass substantive does not present countable units, therefore forcing distinctions on "much" or "little," instead of "many" or "few."

The sequence of prayers and ceremonies constitutes the commemorative sacrifice under the appearance of bread and wine.

They collectively make one body or quantity, often of considerable musical size.

The value of the mass of a body is a function of its velocity with reference to an observer.

For some persons, tuberculosis, hepatitis, malaria, measles or cholera is a velocity.

The masses of their bodies would be inversely proportional to the velocities which a given force imparts to them in a given time.

When he fell down the stairs (x), she was punished for laughing.

The result of this process is often called the weight of the body (y).

A broken body could be obtained by dividing the object of the mass by its audibility.

The greater the object's inaudibility, the more difficult to be moved by its x or its y.

Drum   Bone   Fluid   Hair

I

What pigment, what vehicle, what any two drops reflecting off the visible, what word you must take alone. I thought it was a cast many times repeated, said to be "of" in sunlight falling more or less brightly over the crabapple, what *were* its Cupid and skull. It shouldn't have been blooming, something in charge told the synapses to move to the middle, something in charge told the synapses to move on. What "I am not a mindreader," what Van Eyck only with two hands. If he could get it to bend over, walls, woodwork, what any chance would not remain uncaused. Avoid contact with the eyes. Avoid contact with the skin. She spreads it over the surface until it dries. Something from the lungs has to meet it, in giving up the tension of the personal will, what speak now, what forever hold your, what is to asunder as to forever what it was before.

II

Brush   brush   brush

Rose-red underwing in flight. Yellow-red underwing, in flight. Even on the deepest day, the air between us, How do I look? How do I look? Beside yourself then, smiling, up. Elsewhere, to give others an example, we cut off feet and hands. Is his majesty free at that hour, each style pressing a certain kind of line. It was behave. It was fill with water. It was O O O, a barrelful of amaranths, O O O a barrelful of buoys. On the ground where you lean to look, a Good St. Clare lurks, shoeless. See her run. See her in lower case, slide. On one kind day, in the manner of. Let go her absence of periodicity. Let go three casts of the die. Let go her page falls open to "Fish Magic." Let go this is the place of the black geese that never arrive.

Stroke   stroke   stroke

III

Miss, bring into this body, where form is the distribution of, I accuse myself of memory as a progession of value, like three to five patches of birdsfoot formulating a pathway from the retina to the brain. Where floating fescue, where sea oat, where you do not go gently down that stream. Where misericord, where mens agitat molem, would you bring into this body, Miss form, Miss the distribution of, morula, misurato, on the banks where you sat, remembering. Row, row, row, Miss blanket, Miss blenny, Miss so natural you can't see. If he balances them against one another perfectly, will you do nothing when you hear from me. Where holophrasis. Where aspergillum. Where union by the second or third degree. It's been six months since my last. Where water bearer. Where water softener. Where water ring.

I

Here is your eye. Here are the alleles which give color to your eye, the mixed routes of reference, the million times more than anybody could ever be missed. Flock. The idea of flock. Hundreds of agitated birds swooping over the bridge. Our blessèd moments. Shapes of soft parts, a quantifiable relation to objects, we turn now to your vitreous humor. Shut the lights off, turn the meat down, cover your head. I started doing my duty. Graphs of a dancer's movements. Ten sections of a neural issue. As from air to the cornea. Who in the person is larval or asexual. Who in the person will sit in. Hachure. A parallel walk. From one density to a different density. I was you, once. Come, come, under your skin. In the body receiving itself or its analogies. The my. The bow down before you. White pine to white pine. White pine to redwing to lantern fish.

II

She was full.

She was full with it.

III

and then though

through though

and then through the loop just made

IV

Believe it or not I would swap his desire to see patterns gathering.
Believe it or not we set off several long-haired bodies. Believe it or not
that was the whole of our aestivation. Believe it or not stop talking
about me as if I were not in the room. Pop open a new one. The
developing figure was a monk bent over. Come allow us to see the
sower sow. She contested the waters. Get thee behind. Something in
her eye kept giving you the needle. Something in her eye kept falling
out of line. Believe it or not three persons in one shadow. Believe it or
not could you spare a mind. It clawed each thing as if a temporal
sequence. It clawed each thing as if a temporal w/hole. Believe it or
not six or eight ways of counting on your reticence. Believe it or not
these long thin rods and the wider cones.

I

The end of the rope around the rope

II

Sawhorse

Tubelike human

It was a huge house. Your face has over

I

In this order of magnitude, could you inhabit it. Could you reach up there and inhabit it. In the sorcerer's story, where the soul was in an egg, in a bird, in a box, in a larger bird. You removed your soul to prevent you from saying it. There, there, remove your soul. There, you, remove it. There as you were removing, another bird. You were not supposed to say another bird, but you were saying it. Could you step back. Could you step back from under cover and render it. There, there, in the coverbird. In there under cover, bird, sleep. There's a good, there's a good coverbird. Let the shepherd who along with his sheep. They are spoken. They are spoken for. They are spoken with. Therein, let there in, let there you be. Could you have seen your look when I said spoken, when I said spoken for, when I said therein let therein let there you me.

II

Little lamb who

Little lamb who

III

Methods using functional magnetic resonance. Methods using a hollow newel arc. Methods using Avicenna. Methods using vastly more than the sum of its parts. You put your right hand in. You put your right hand out. Fleece. Sore mouth. Hoof rot. Correlates of mental states, the laps of the participants, the body in question that doesn't make a sound. What if methods using come hither. What if methods using wwwdot thigh. What if methods addressing the middle as the middle, a position untenable, like one leg twined around the rungs of the chair he tied me to with vines. There it flows, there it goes, like hollie point lace, through what, which, where, when, why. Vanishing points. A fault block mountain. A fumbling tent worm. Owning it, owning "I." What if methods using wwwdot wrestling. What if methods using wwwdot lye.

1.

I concede the field. I concede the bindweed near the field.

She bends down to emulate the formulations of a walk.

The question of where the temperature of a binding body falls.

Of a color, risqué. Of a face, the pressure to go round the other side of the porch.

In mixed company who benefits.

You see the crescent sweep "as" harbor to cliffs, "as" looking north.

Blue back, blue bishop, blue bice, one life on top of another life, the picture of him she took, Block Island, Spring House, double exposed.

What in life would you exchange for no oil.

Use with a preceding so or such. Look up life. Look up oil.

According to Thackeray, the ladies were very blue and well-informed.

He says he is going to open up some of the B & B you bought.

According to that which, the way to which. Imperfect chamber. Mock vulnerability. Blue mud. Blue mouth fish. Blue north.

2.

Billing period: current billing period: please print: please mail to: current charges: current usage charge: current distribution charge: current meter reading: current distribution adjustment: previous distribution adjustment: current customer service: previous customer service: office location: previous office location: never worried about the condition of the Iraqi people before. Payments balance forwarded: payments previous balance forwarded: therm factor: local therm factor: oil of the sick: received: oil of the catechumens received: walk-ins: total walk-ins: customer number: customer premise number: other premise number: equinox: vernal equinox: other: your big and little punishments. Current lymphatic systems: current respiratory systems: current male reproductive and urinary systems: delivery vehicle: diastolic delivery vehicle: account number: due date: previous due date: Mohamed Atta: previous Mohamed Atta: previous your boy my boy. Linseed: oil of linseed: oil with ink: oil with metered readings: rough winds do shake: procoagulants: three: anticoagulants: six: therm factor: total therm factor: total cost of costs.

3.

Chorus:
        windy too, lumen etc.

4.

The Policy Office Electricity Modeling System (POEMS) is an integrated energy model of the United States with a specific focus on the electric sector.

"Whatever you say" may imply a disposition in your person to resist some-one in an electric sector, for example, one who could be smarting in the sun or, likewise, glowing.

To own eyes, even crude eyes, alas, from one day to the next, an overlook.

A cost/benefit analyst is affected by the planner's paradox, so that in a non-regulatory landscape he appoints, dying mother to the background, insult in the manner of an overlook.

The challenge for the policymaker is to characterize as accurately as possible the direct, intended consequences of a policy measure and its indirect perhaps unintended consequences, imperial conduct to ohm, ampere, *ars poetica*.

The POEMS model incorporates an integrated multi-market model that uses a constrained bilateral transaction framework, so he may think others are naturally obligated to step aside if perhaps he tells them to.

The bottom line is not what's best but a hurdle rate.

So what if what the brain is programmed to believe or not believe, escort like a tug on the river, departing water figure to each degree of its separation, constitutes her bidding behavior.

Fuels said my muse to me, meaning March, April.

The effect of the former is a transmission constraint, steep hill down to the bike path, your turn, not your turn, water mobilizing at its surface, air, oil length, lucrum cessans, I bid you the angles between various faces of a crystal.

Changing the motor features of the regulatory landscape inevitably triggers such unanticipated cause-and-effect sequences, "about face" away from the pressure by the tug, water motive small medium large, impending death to the size of an interior.

She says it: thieves took everything.

He bullies her.

Fill the air as you are filled, as she is filled, speech not for its content but for its connective properties, huge amounts of motion spent in motion, "about" as heart as congested figure as contiguity, current projected outcome as fragile as a motherline: mouth to face, face to spirit, mouth to vacuity.

5.

source:

Had, having, and in quest to have

6.

Renewable   nonrenewable

I called you names, for the further processing of color or movement, all you were able to get into, a sort of blur. She leaned out against the water. Lay me down like anthozoa to anthozoa, with the other light things that brush against the earth. Breathe. Don't breathe. Breathe. A figure in a constellation was staring off. Did it turn up three days later, did it accept inside its body, a no for universal application, an only mine or yours? Gate One. Open your mouth. If you would only open your mouth. Gate Two. To bridle, to curb, to dam. Gate Three. Anagnorisis. Gate Four. Closed. Gate Five. Hold up. Gate Six. If everywhere that Mary went, the brain was public and exposed. Gate Seven. Do you mind, do you. Gate Eight. Fish moving in the boat's direction will be recorded in our diagram with the more substantial marks. Gate Nine. The rhythm and interval between objects. Gate Ten. Our simplest subject. Our lightest lights. Our darkest darks.

When the ropes broke. First, the feeling of a propositional. Then the moon as discursive prose. P A T pat. M A T mat. R A T rat. Snapping them in certain places in order to accentuate their holes. Temporal to spatial, your mouthparts. Temporal to spatial your mouthparts, before a map-like body, enclosed. Blessèd are the forecasters. Like little legs running from your mouthparts, blessèd are the forecasters, running to and fro.

Wait up. It is goose o'clock. It is goose with eleven minutes past. Do you have a moment to go over. Do you have a moment to keep your eyes on the road. If the space is limited as in the retina. Can you do it a little more lightly. Can you do it a little more: slow. What is it that announces rent conditions. Let the records show.

The "lovely ropemaker" in "In Nomine" is a reference to the poet Louise Labé. "If all the trees were one tree" is from the *Oxford Book of Nursery Rhymes*.

The poem "Introibo" adds to and deranges material found in Rebecca Rupp's book *Committed to Memory*.

The phrase *judica me* in "Psalm" can be translated as "do me justice" or "judge me." "Ballast love" is from John Donne's "Air and Angels."

The last two quotations in "Gloria" are from William James, *The Varieties of Religious Experience.*

"Audrey Meadows' elbow" in "Epistle 1" is a reference to the way stage directions could be given in *The Honeymooners.* An excessive use of the letter "m" is an obscure definition for "mimmation."

According to the *Oxford Dictionary of the English Language,* epistemic modality (in "Epistle 3") refers to a judgment about the truth of a proposition (whether it is possible, probable, or necessarily true). Deontic modality involves giving directives in terms of permission and obligation. Phoebe, a deacon in the early Church, carried Paul's Epistle to the Romans.

The quotation in the first "Recitative" is from an essay by Michael Rock.

Most of the language in the second "Recitative," with additions and varying degrees of modification, has been taken from the following sources: *The Family Medical Dictionary, The World Book Encyclopedia, The Columbia Encyclopedia, The New York Public Library Science Desk Reference, The Oxford Dictionary,* and *The American Heritage Dictionary.*

"A fault block mountain" and "a fumbling tent worm" in "Agnus Dei" are borrowed from George Johnson's *Fire in the Mind: Science, Faith, and the Search for Order.*

Approximately one quarter of the language in Section 4 of "Domine, Non Sum Dignus" was taken (some of it verbatim or nearly verbatim) from a report posted on the U.S. Department of Energy's website: "Report to Congress: Impacts of the Federal Energy Regulatory Commission's Proposal for Standard Market Design" (April 30, 2003). "Had, having, and in quest to have" is from Shakespeare's Sonnet 129.

The sentence "fish moving in the boat's direction..." in "Communion" is based on a sentence from *The Domain of Images* by James Elkins.

ABOUT THE AUTHOR:

Catherine Imbriglio was born in Massachusetts and has lived most of her life in Rhode Island. She received an MA in creative writing (poetry) and a Ph.D. in American literature from Brown University. Her poetry and criticism have appeared in *American Letters & Commentary, Caliban, Conjunctions, Contemporary Literature, Denver Quarterly, Epoch, First Intensity, New American Writing, No: A Journal of the Arts, Pleiades, WebConjunctions* and elsewhere. A selection of her poetry is available in *The Iowa Anthology of New American Poetries*, ed. Reginald Shepherd. She is a recipient of an Untermeyer fellowship in poetry and a merit award in poetry from the RI State Council on the Arts. She teaches in the Expository Writing Program at Brown.

This book was designed and computer typeset by Rosmarie Waldrop in 10 pt. Palatino and Phyllis initials. Printed on 55 lb. Writers' Natural (an acid-free paper), smyth-sewn and glued into paper covers by McNaughton & Gunn in Saline, Michigan. The cover uses a detail of aquatint #2 from "7 Black Poems" by Irene A. Lawrence.

There are 1000 copies, of which 50 are numbered & signed.